I0417776

Learning to Just Be Thankful

by

TERRI JOHNSON

ILLUSTRATIONS BY JASON FOWLER

the PeppertreePress, LLC
www.peppertreepublishing.com

Copyright © Terri Johnson, 2014

All rights reserved. Published by the Peppertree Press, LLC.
the Peppertree Press and associated logos are trademarks of
the Peppertree Press, LLC.
No part of this publication may be reproduced, stored in a retrieval
system, transmitted in any form or by any means, electronic, mechanical,
photocopying, recording, or otherwise, without prior written permission
of the publisher and author/illustrator.
Graphic design by Rebecca Barbier.

For information regarding permission,
call 941-922-2662 or contact us at our website:
www.peppertreepublishing.com or write to:
the Peppertree Press, LLC.
Attention: Publisher
1269 First Street, Suite 7
Sarasota, Florida 34236

ISBN: 978-1-61493-256-7

Library of Congress Number: 2014907218

Printed in the U.S.A.

Second printing September 2019

Hi, my name is Terri Johnson. My children inspired me to write this book. Their thoughts and words were heard, and they meant a lot to me. Parents, this was a lesson because sometimes we give our kids so much through love, attention, and materials things yet then fail to teach them the important values of life. One thing in particular is to just be thankful. So this book was written to teach our kids that there are others in worse situations than we are, yet they are still very thankful.

FOOD

Good afternoon, Grammy!

Good afternoon, Zay!

I had a great day at school today.

> You did?

> Yes, and guess what?

> What, honey?

> I stayed on green all day.

> Oh wow!

> That's awesome dude!

> But, Grammy!

> Yes.

4

We only had a lunchable today,
and I didn't get full.

Well, at least you had
food for lunch, right?

Right, Grammy.

Give thanks in all circumstances

5

Let Grammy tell you something. Do you know that there are many people in the world that won't get any food today?

Yes, Grammy, you tell me that all the time.

So guess what, Zay?

What, Grammy?

Just say thank you every chance you get. Just say thank you that you had food for lunch today.

You're right, Grammy. I will learn to do that, because at least I had food and I don't want to know how it will feel not to eat.

You right, Zay. Grammy loves you and your heart.

Let us be thankful

CLOTHES

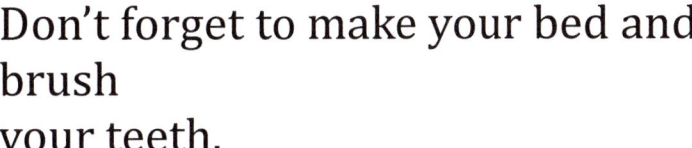

Good morning, Mommy!

Good morning, Calvee! Time to get

ready for school

Yes, Mommy

Don't forget to make your bed and brush
your teeth.

Yes, Mommy

All finished!

Great! Now lotion yourself and put on your clothes and shoes.

Yes, ma'am

Mommy.

Yes.

Give thanks in all circumstances

It's a boy in my class whose shoe has a hole in it and his jacket is too little.

It is?

Yes.

Well, what do you think we should do, Calvee?

Well, Mommy. We can go through my clothes and shoes to see if I have an extra jacket and a pair of shoes.

Calvee, that's a wonderful idea. When you come home from school today with Grammy, we will sit down and go through your stuff.

Okay, Mommy.

Yes---! School is out. I can't wait to get home.

Good afternoon, Grammy!

Good afternoon, Calvee!

Guess what? Guess what?

What, Calvee?

Mommy and I are going to go through my clothes and shoes today.

Really, why?

I asked Mommy so that I can give it to my friend in my class.

That's awesome of you! God will bless you for being so kind and having a heart like that.

Grammy, I feel sad for him.

Why?

Because I dress nice all the time and I want him to dress nice too.

Oh, that is sweet of you. Grammy and Mommy are so proud of you.

I will give thanks to Him in song

I'm home, Mommy!

How was your day, Calvee?

It was good.

That's awesome. Keep up the good work.

Mommy, are you ready?

Yes, but you want a snack or sandwich?

No, Mommy, I can wait till we are finished.

Okay.

We went into Calvee's room. Then we sat down and picked through the clothes and shoes.

Mommy and I found him five pants, five shirts, two pairs of shoes and a jacket.

Yes—! I am so happy, Mommy.

Me too, Calvee.

I can't wait to give it to him.

You have to wait till I talk to his mom first.

Okay, Mommy.

So we went to meet his friend and mother at the park.

Hi, Friend!

Hi, Calvee!

I have a big surprise for you.

What? What?

Now you can look cool like me.

Here are some pants, shirts, shoes, and a jacket for you.

Yeah! Cool, Calvee! Thank you, Calvee, give me a hug.

You are my best friend. Thank you—see you tomorrow.

Give thanks to the Lord for His unfailing love...

Be Thankful!

Mommy, I learned something.

What?

I learned to just be thankful, because I got a lot of clothes and shoes. And sometimes other people don't have what I do.

That's right, Calvee.

Learn to just be thankful.

A PLACE TO STAY

Mother!

Yes, Laylay.

I wish we had a bigger house.

Well, Laylay, we have a four-bedroom home.

I know, but we need a bigger house.

Why is that?

So that we can get more stuff.

I don't understand, why you would need more stuff and more rooms?

Are you not thankful we have this?

Yeah—! But.

Hold the but.

13

Let's take a trip.

Where are we going?

You will see, get your brothers and come to the truck.

Mommy, where are we going? Where are we driving to?

Mommy! Mommy!

OK, just look. This is a shelter. See all the people outside?

Asleep on the side of the road, asleep under the bridge? See them pushing a grocery cart down the street with all the things they have?

Is it a lot of stuff in the cart that they can live off day-to-day?

No, Mom, we have more than them.

So let me ask you the question again. Why do you need more, when these people have little and they are thankful?

Mom, we are sad. Why?

Because we have more and we have a place to stay, and they don't.

15

So does it make you wonder?

Wonder for what?

Do you think that it's OK to keep wanting, when people who don't have a lot are still thankful?

No, it's not right and it makes us look greedy and unthankful.

So what do you suggest?

We just need to learn to be thankful for what we have now, because tomorrow it's not promised to us.

16

LIFE & FAMILY

Hi, Mommy. Hi, Grammy.

Hi, Moe! How are you?

I'm good.

That's great, Moe.

Mommy, Grammy, I'm just so thankful.

Why? Thankful for what?

For one because I'm living, I lived to see
age 14, we have a nice place to stay,
plenty of food, clothes, and shoes.
We have a bed to sleep in and a vehicle to ride in.

You know, Mommy, thank you for showing us where we could be, because I realize that we sometimes complain instead of just being thankful. So many people—adults and children—don't have what we have and they are more thankful than we are.

We have a great family, and we need to learn to just get along, no matter what. All families have many ups and downs, but if we keep our faith and believe in God, all things are possible. But if we look at our situations closely and examine it well, we will always see that someone is in a worse situation than we are. So just learn to be thankful and many blessings will follow.

Granny Last Said To Me

Don't Give Up On God

www.ingramcontent.com/pod-product-compliance
Lightning Source LLC
Chambersburg PA
CBHW060831290526
45792CB00005BB/1879